Slumpbuster: A Battle Tested 5-Step System to Breakout of Slumps

Copyright © 2024 by Brandon Guyer

All rights reserved.

Permission to reproduce or transmit in any form or by any means, electronic or mechanical, including photocopying, photographic and recording audio or video, or by any information storage and retrieval system, must be obtained in writing from the author.

Slumpbuster: A Battle Tested 5-Step System to Breakout of Slumps is a registered trademark of Brandon Guyer.

First printing June 2024

Slumpbuster: A Battle Tested 5-Step System to Breakout of Slumps / by Brandon Guyer

Paperback ISBN: 9798328535656

Printed in the U.S.A.

TABLE OF CONTENTS

→ Introduction — Page 1

→ Step 1: Master the Fundamentals — Page 3

→ Step 2: Accept What Is — Page 8

→ Step 3: Detach From Results — Page 11

→ Step 4: Attach to Controllables — Page 12

→ Step 5: Pre-Pitch Routine — Page 14

→ 5 Bonus Tips to Break Out of a Slump — Page 16

→ Summary — Page 24

ABOUT THE AUTHOR

BRANDON GUYER

I feel blessed to say I'm a 7 year veteran of Major League Baseball. It's something I am very proud of. Of course I would have loved to play 20+ years, but it wasn't in the cards, and I'm at peace with that.

When I sit back and reflect on what I could have done differently, I can honestly say there's nothing. I gave my all every single day and earned everything I was able to achieve. My scholarship to the University of Virginia, my promotions in the minor leagues, my call to the show, my role as a player in the bigs. I worked for literally everything.

Today I'm better for it. I'm grateful for the demotions and the promotions. I'm grateful for the strike outs and the home runs, for the hits I got robbed of and the ones that blooped in. I'm grateful for the losses and the wins, the struggles and the triumphs, the successes and failures. I'm grateful for the joy and the tears, and for the beginning and the end. I'm grateful for all of that because now I have the experience and knowledge to pass onto ballplayers of all ages.

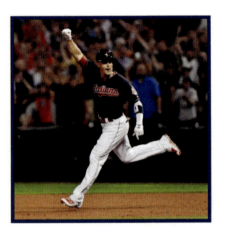

Introduction

Imagine standing at the plate, feeling confidence radiate through your body. You see the pitch perfectly, your swing is smooth, and the ball jumps off your bat.

Every at-bat, every pitch, you're in the zone. You're delivering for your team, contributing to the win, and your stats reflect your hard work and dedication. The season progresses, and your consistency makes you a massive part of your team's success.

This is what it feels like when you're full of confidence and skilled at preventing slumps.

Now, picture the opposite. Pitches seem faster, your swing feels off, and every at-bat is a struggle. The more you try to break out of the slump, the deeper you sink.

Frustration builds, affecting not just your performance, but your love for the game. The season feels endless, you start to doubt your abilities, and it only gets worse as each game passes.

This is what it's like when your confidence is shattered and you fail to prevent slumps.

This book is your guide to avoiding the second scenario. It's a step-by-step system designed to help you prevent slumps before they start, and quickly snap out of them when they do.

It's the same system I used while playing Major League Baseball for close to a decade and the same system thousands of ballplayers of all ages have used as well.

This book isn't just a few tips for you to try out and hope for the best. It's a system. A system that, if followed in the exact way I lay out, is guaranteed to put you in the best position possible to lead you to the results you're looking for.

As a bonus, I will also share 5 ways to instantly snap out of a slump. So, when they come, you know how to bounce back fast full of confidence, making each slump shorter than the last.

What this book doesn't include is a promise you will never slump again. Slumps are inevitable. They will happen to you – no matter how strong your mind is or how physically talented you are.

The good news is, all you have to do is follow this system, step by step, and the way you play this game will change forever.

Are you ready to unlock your potential and become the player you've always wanted to be? Let's dive in.

Step 1 - Master the Fundamentals

The first step to preventing slumps has nothing to do with your mechanics. It actually has nothing to do with baseball at all.

The first step is to master the fundamentals of life. These fundamentals will lead to you becoming mentally stronger and more energized than you've ever been in your life.

It all starts with knowing that your **physiology** (your body) drives your **psychology** (your mind) WAY more than you think. The more energized you are, the better you will handle the inevitable setbacks, challenges, and obstacles that come your way in your career.

I don't say this lightly: Getting more mentally and physically energized than you've ever been in your life is the **#1 lever you can pull on for your success both ON and OFF the field**. It will give you a TRUE edge over the competition.

The 5 universal fundamentals of elite performers in life are:

1. **Eating**
2. **Sleeping**
3. **Training (Physically & Mentally)**
4. **Breathing**
5. **Self-Discipline**

From my experience and perspective, there is no way any athlete will ever tap into their true potential without having these fundamentals dialed in.

Each of these five fundamentals affects how you think. How you think determines how you approach each at-bat, and how you approach each at-bat is what determines what happens.

There may be players on your team who eat a lot of junk food, stay up all night playing video games, and don't know the first thing about breathwork – yet they still dominate. Trust me when I say, that won't last forever. That also doesn't mean you can or should do that too.

One thing I learned in my career is the further you go in this game, the more each advantage you have over other players matters. And since most players aren't taking these fundamentals seriously enough – if you do – you will instantly gain an edge over your competition.

Know that greatness is CONSISTENCY with the fundamentals. Let me quickly explain each of them:

1) Eating

Picture your body as a racecar. How you eat is the fuel for your engine. If you focus on eating high protein meals, quality whole foods, healthy carbs & fats, and limiting sugar as much as possible (especially in drinks), you will have more energy, focus, and success on the field. That's a guarantee.

Here are 6 eating principles to follow:

- Keep it simple
- More real food, less processed food
- Drink and eat less sugar
- Have a clean environment
- Find what works best for you
- Real food before supplements

TAKE-ACTION STEP: What is the #1 change you could make to the way you eat that YOU KNOW would make the biggest impact? There's no better day than today to make that change!

2) Sleeping

The #1 performance enhancer - a good night of sleep. It is scientifically proven that consistent, quality sleep leads to:

- Overall better well-being
- Increased strength and speed
- Better decision making
- Better recovery
- Quicker reaction times
- Less injuries
- Longer playing career (a study proved this in MLB players!)

Here's 3 tips to improve your sleep so that you can "out sleep" the competition:

1) BE IN BED FOR 8 - 10 HOURS

Aim for at least 7-8 hours of actual sleep per night. To do that, shoot for 8-10 hours in bed because it may take you longer to actually fall asleep, and you'll spend time tossing and turning during the night. Understand that a good day today started the night before with a good night of sleep!

2) LIMIT INPUTS BEFORE BED

Limiting inputs and blue light from screens is VERY important for overall sleep quality. You should aim to put your phone and other devices away at least 30-60 minutes before you go to sleep. This will help you fall asleep quicker and also STAY asleep. The less inputs and stimulation on your brain the better QUALITY sleep you will get.

3) HAVE A GREAT SLEEP ENVIRONMENT

TEMPERATURE: Studies have found the optimal temperature is 61 - 68 degrees. Experiment to find what temperature helps you sleep best and deepest.

NOISE: Block out unnecessary noise like cars driving outside, a noisy neighbor or anything you can think of. There are many devices and apps on your phone that produce soothing, ambient white noise that will help you get uninterrupted sleep.

LIGHT: "Light proof" your room. This can be as simple as wearing an eye mask or buying blackout shades for your windows if necessary.

PS: My secret weapon to recharge before competition was NSDR: Non-Sleep Deep Rest. This is where you simply "turn off" your brain and body for 5-20 minutes pre-game. Find a quiet place, close your eyes, and focus on your breath. Trust me, it is a GAME-CHANGER.

TAKE-ACTION STEP: What is the #1 change you could make to the way you sleep that YOU KNOW would make the biggest impact? There's no better day than today to make that change!

3) Training (Physically & Mentally)

Physical Skills + Mental Skills = Your True Potential Unlocked.

Physical training: Work hard and smart. Understand where you need to get stronger, explosive, and mobile. Recover properly after each workout. Hire a coach to help you stay on track if you struggle to stay consistent. Hit baseball specific body parts like core, lower body, and forearms.

Mental training: Think of going to the 'Mind Gym' to intentionally train your mind for at least 1% of your day (14 minutes and 24 seconds is 1% of a day). Below are some powerful exercises you can do in the 'Mind Gym':

- Breathwork / Meditation
- Visualization
- Journaling
- Daily gratitude practice
- Read mental performance books
- Listen to a mindset podcast (I'm bias, but the daily MLM podcast is a good one!)
- Do something uncomfortable (cold shower, cardio, mobility, stretching, etc.)
- Concentration grids
- DWYSYWD: Do What You Say You Will Do

These are the kind of exercises we focus on in the Major League Mindset program – my 8-week Online Training Program. I'll give you more details on that later.

TAKE-ACTION STEP: What is the #1 change you could make to the way you train that YOU KNOW would make the biggest impact? There's no better day than today to make that change!

4) Breathing

How you breathe is scientifically proven to affect how you perform on the field. Unfortunately, most players either don't know how important it is, or don't care to learn. I understand why – it seems like such a small thing – but in this game, the small changes are what lead to big changes.

The next time the game is speeding up on you and you're losing emotional control, bring your focus back to the present-moment by having **AOB** (awareness of breath). In other words, be aware of and notice the air coming in as you inhale and out as you exhale. Give this a try between pitches and tell me if you don't feel drastically different. I'll be very surprised if I hear from you.

Scan this code for a video of me explaining everything you'll ever need to know to maximize the impact of your breath, or what I like to call a 'Big League Breath'.

TAKE-ACTION STEP: What is the #1 change you could make to the way you utilize your breath that YOU KNOW would make the biggest impact? There's no better day than today to make that change!

5) Self-Discipline

Self-Discipline is all about doing what you know is best for you, whether you feel like it or not. Another way to put it is this: Put your actions over your feelings and **DWYSYWD** (Do What You Say You Will Do).

It's easy to be disciplined when things are going good, but TRUE self-mastery is the WORSE things are going, the MORE committed and the MORE disciplined you are. This is one of the best ways to build confidence – leading to less slumps.

TAKE-ACTION STEP: What is the #1 change you could make to your self-discipline that YOU KNOW would make the biggest impact? There's no better day than today to make that change!

Step 2 - Accept What Is

What is a slump?

A slump is not getting the results you want for an extended period of time.

A lack of results for a long enough time leads to your confidence being shattered, which is a big reason why you find yourself in a slump. It's why your coach has to move you down in the lineup. It's why your favorite game on the planet becomes your largest source of frustration.

This is what a slump is – but it isn't what a slump has to be.

Instead of being afraid of them, **accept** them. You must embrace reality in order to improve it. Being frustrated by slumps means you care and want to compete – that's a good thing and how it should be.

But when you don't expect slumps to happen or are overly emotional about being in one – this leads to more self-doubt and keeps you stuck in the downward spiral of a slump longer than necessary.

If you **accept** slumps as part of the game, you will build the "mental stamina" to not let them affect you as much, which in turn will allow you to snap out of them faster.

Quick story:

When I was going through THE WORST slump of my life back in 2009 while playing with the Double-A Tennessee Smokies (I was hitting a whopping .190 after 200 at-bats), I was taught to accept these 3 universal 'Truths of Life' by a mentor:

1. You will deal with **ADVERSITY**
2. You will have **UNCERTAINTY** of your future
3. It will take **CONSTANT WORK** and **DISCIPLINE** to achieve your goals

Embracing these 3 truths allowed me to snap out of that slump, finish the season strong, and then earn the Cubs Minor League Player of the Year award the very next season. (image below)

Once I truly ACCEPTED adversity, uncertainty, constant work/discipline, and realized that I couldn't avoid them, everything changed. I enjoyed the game more than ever, and started to play free & loose more consistently.

The same can happen to you once you realize that being in a slump doesn't mean anything is wrong with you or your swing. It happens to everyone.

A slump is nothing more than a sign you're a human being striving for greatness while playing a very hard game, and adversity (slumps) and uncertainty of your future are all parts of the process.

Again: You MUST accept reality (rather than fight against it) in order to improve it!

Two other gems I learned that year:

1) If you're not getting the outcomes you want, it's because it's the challenge you need. Believe that this struggle is happening **'for you'** not **'to you'**.

2) It's funny how quickly baseball can turn around if you keep pushing forward and expecting things to be most difficult right before they get drastically better.

Winning the 2009 Cubs Minor League POY Award

PLEASE remember this the next time you feel as if you can't catch a break or you start to question if you will ever get back to being the hitter you know you can be.

Final point on this: how you view slumps drastically affects your self-image – AKA how you view yourself. You are only as good as what you believe you're capable of. Trust me, you can't outperform your self image. How you view yourself determines how you think, act, play, and live your life.

Having self-compassion and being kind to yourself during tough stretches is HUGE to preserve your self-image. Speak to yourself as you would a young kid who is struggling.

A great way to do this is by asking yourself, "Is how I'm talking to myself HELPFUL or HURTFUL?" If hurtful, immediately shift your self-talk!

This is one more reason why **ACCEPTING** slumps is necessary and powerful.

TAKE-ACTION STEP: Write down the 3 'Truths of Life' on a piece of paper and put that piece of paper somewhere you can see it as a constant reminder to you. I can't emphasize the importance of this enough!

Step 3 - Detach from Results

One of the main reasons you may find yourself lacking confidence and in a slump is because you are attached to results. You're relying on something you don't have control over (results) for confidence, rather than basing your confidence off of what is 100% in your control (your preparation, responses, effort, attitude, etc.)

Even if you do everything right, getting a hit is outside of your control. That's why you get frustrated. Even if you're not worried about getting a hit, you may be focused on the other team, the umpire, or something outside of the game. Nothing hurts your performance more than misplaced focus.

To be fair, I don't blame you. I remember times going into games knowing my batting average before every game, doing the math in my head for how many hits I "needed" to get my average where I wanted it. It's natural to care, because as hitters – we are judged by our batting average.

Which is why I'm not saying your average isn't important. It is. What I'm saying is, your attachment to your average or other factors outside of your control is the main reason you're slumping.

When we focus on what's out of our control, that very thing then controls us and drains our confidence.

Interestingly enough – the best way to increase your average is to detach from results and not focus on your average at all.

Instead, you need to focus on what is 100% in your control, which brings us to Step 4...

Step 4 - Attach to Controllables

Even with perfect timing, great mechanics, and a rock-solid approach, you can't control if you're going to get a hit because the other team, umpires, etc., have a say as well. So, what what can you focus on?

QAB's: Quality At-Bats

Having a quality at-bat is 100% in your control. Examples of a QAB are:

1. Hard contact (no matter the outcome)
2. Walks
3. Hit by pitches
4. Long at-bats (7+ pitches)
5. RBIs
6. Moving the runner
7. Sacrifice fly and/or bunt

I may be missing a few, but you get the point. There's a lot of ways to have a quality at-bat, which is another reason it's a better goal than simply "getting a hit".

Another benefit of focusing on quality at-bats over hits is where you shift your focus to. When you're focused on quality ABs, you shift the focus away from yourself (internal) and onto your team (external).

You're in the box focused on doing your job and helping your team win. That selfless approach to hitting is what every coach wants. It's also a great way to remove any pressure you have on yourself – and less pressure usually leads to more success.

Just like your swing, QAB's can be trained. Challenge yourself to work on situational hitting in the cage and on the field at practice. Push yourself.

Working on your swing isn't about hitting bombs and seeing how high you can get your exit velo. It's about getting your swing and mind ready to produce in the game – and training QAB's is the best way to do that.

Then after the game, evaluate your performance based on the QUALITY OF YOUR AT BATS, not the outcomes. Ask yourself, "Did I do everything I needed to put myself in the best position to have more QAB's?" This is where the 5 Hitting Checkpoints are HUGE (explained in video and graphic linked below).

If you were 0-4 but had 3 quality at bats, chalk that up as a great day at the plate! Your ability to have quality at-bats (in your control) then becomes the basis for your confidence instead of your results (out of your control). **CONTROL THE CONTROLLABLES!!**

Lastly, know that the key to successful hitting is **contact point**. By following everything we're covering in this book, you will:

- Slow the game and your mind down
- Get to a consistent **contact point**
- Put yourself in the best position to have more quality at bats, which will lead to more hits and more of the results you're after!

Below you'll find two videos and two graphics. One is to help you get clarity on what is 100% in your control and what is not, and the other goes over the 5 Hitting Checkpoints that will lead you to more QAB's.

Scan here for the 'Control the Controllables' Video / Graphic

Scan here for the 5 Hitting Checkpoints Video / Graphic

TAKE-ACTION STEP: Start keeping track of your QAB average. Do so by writing in a journal after each at bat and/or each game. Base your confidence off of this average, NOT your batting average.

Step 5 - Pre-Pitch Routine

Now that you know what you're trying to accomplish in the box, you are ready for the final step of this system:

Develop a Pre-Pitch Routine.

It's not enough to know what you want to do in the box – you need to have a process you can follow to get your mind right before every single pitch.

A step-by-step plan that gets your mind focused and stacks the odds in your favor. Think of your pre-pitch routine as a "cheat code" to slow the game down and put you one step ahead of your competition.

This routine will help you WIN the most important time during a game: **the time in between pitches**. This is the time we want to be in total control of ourselves. Think about it. Between each pitch, what do you say to yourself? How are you breathing? What are you focused on?

In my experience playing and coaching thousands of players, most players don't take control during this time. They are letting their thoughts happen by chance and are just thinking about whatever comes to mind. They definitely aren't "winning" this time. Do you do the same?

If so, a pre-pitch routine will be a game-changer for you. Using that time to encourage yourself, lock in on the task at hand, and take a powerful breath will give you the best chance for success.

It will also prevent you from overthinking, getting in your head about a bad swing, or upset with an umpire's call. With a routine, you just follow each step in between every pitch and let it naturally prepare your mind and body for the task at hand.

In a way, your pre-pitch routine "tricks" your mind into treating every pitch like a fresh opportunity to do damage. It directs your focus to what you WANT to happen (hit the ball hard), rather than what you DON'T WANT to happen (get out, strikeout, look bad, etc.)

It takes you out of an emotional headspace and into a focused, confident state of mind – which is the best way to help you and your team succeed.

Here's the Pre-Pitch Routine I give to all athletes as part of the Major League Mindset program:

Scan this QR Code to watch a video explaining the MLM Pre-Pitch Routine

To maximize the power of your routine, you first need to spend some time developing it. Once you have a routine you like, trust it – whether things are going your way or not.

You can't allow a bad at-bat, game, or series of games lead to you giving up on your routine. Make adjustments if and when you think you need to, BUT stick with it no matter what happens, and you won't be disappointed in the long run.

You'll notice after a while of doing your routine, you will walk into the box with confidence by default. Your days of relying on hits for confidence will end forever. Wouldn't that be nice?

TAKE-ACTION STEP: Develop your very own pre-pitch routine. Start getting as many reps as you can with it - whether that be at home, in the cages, during practice, during games, in your mind, etc. This is VITAL to you finding out what works best for you so that you can begin to WIN the time in between pitches.

5 BONUS TIPS TO INSTANTLY BREAK OUT OF A SLUMP

You now understand how to prevent slumps. The question becomes: what do you do if you're in the middle of a slump? How do you snap out of it and get back on track fast?

Here's 5 tips I personally used and have taught thousands players like you:

Tip 1 - Shift Your Perspective

When we are struggling, our perspective is usually negative. We are more focused on what we don't have (such as hits lately), rather than what we do have. Because of that, we lose our enjoyment of the game and dread going to the field. One way to help you keep a positive perspective through it all is to appreciate everything, every day. That is where a daily gratitude practice comes in.

Give this a try: Buy a journal and every day for at least the next week write down 2-5 different things you are grateful for in your life. Think of different blessings, gifts, people, experiences, and accomplishments you're thankful for. I promise you this: Gratitude is the quickest way to turn yourself from thinking and feeling **negative** to thinking and feeling **positive**.

Study after study has proven that by simply writing down a few things we are grateful for everyday makes us 25% happier. In no time, you will 100% show up with a different energy about you, you'll find yourself happier, and your current slump will no longer affect you as much.

Let me end this tip with a quote from Darrin Donnelly in his great book **The Mental Game**: *"Don't wait until you accomplish a specific goal before you allow yourself to be thankful. Choose to be grateful right now. By choosing to be grateful, you'll feel better about yourself and the world around you. And when you feel better, you play better. Doesn't matter what it is you're playing, when you feel good about yourself, you perform better. Countless psychological studies have proven this."*

One final thought for this section: Be a great teammate no matter your results. True character shows when people are struggling. Instead of thinking internally about yourself, think externally about how you can help others. Another great way to shift your perspective!

TAKE-ACTION STEP: Every day, starting today, write in a gratitude journal. Keep it short, keep it simple, and avoid 'gratitude fatigue' by writing something different each time…

In fact, let's start right now. What are YOU grateful for? Please take a moment to think about three things you're grateful for:

1. _____
2. _____
3. _____

Repeat. Every single day.

Tip 2 - Define Your Best and Worst Self

In the Major League Mindset Program – we use animals, superheroes, etc., to help us develop self-awareness. As silly as it may sound – start by coming up with and naming the best and worst versions of you. This is very important because we as humans are constantly fighting the internal battle between our best and worst self. When we win that battle, we win the game of life, ON and OFF the field.

A great way for you to get started with this is to think of your **BFS** (Body Language, Focus, Self-Talk) when you're at your best - and at your worst. This exercise (linked below) will help you build self-awareness so that you always know which version of you is in control.

Personally, my best self animal represents the powerful body language, present-moment focus, positive self-talk, fearless, confident and undeniable version of myself, so I chose a Lion.

My worst self animal represents the weak body language, scattered focus, negative self-talk, timid, anxious, and afraid version of myself – so I chose a Sheep.

Scan this QR Code for the BFS & Best/Worst Animal Video / Graphics

TAKE-ACTION STEP: What did you name your best and worst self? Take time to develop the self-awareness needed to know when the best version of you or the worst version of you is in control. You must control yourself to have better control of your performance!

Tip 3 - Flip the Switch

The hardest part of going through a slump is controlling your emotions. To overcome this, you need to learn how to "Flip the Switch". Flipping the switch is going from your worst self to your best self, which is why the best/worst exercise above is VERY important.

Think of flipping the switch as a mental tool that shifts your mind from negative and powerfull to positive and powerful.

When flipping the switch, use the "Three B's" to make it effortless.

Big Body Language: Assume a powerful, warrior-like posture. Your body language is how you carry yourself on the field. After a bad at-bat, are you sulking in the dugout? Or are you standing tall with your head high supporting your teammates?

Focusing on carrying yourself with confidence and power (even if you're frustrated) is key to breaking out of a slump.

Big League Breath: Take a slow, deep, meaningful breath to reset your mind and connect with the most confident version of yourself. This is scientifically proven to reduce stress and anxiety immediately. As you're inhaling, imagine flipping on a light switch in your mind.

Bring It On: Turn fear into fuel by repeating to yourself "Bring It On." Scared of striking out? Bring It On. Nervous in a high-pressure situation? Bring It On. Swing not feeling the best? Bring It On.

These three words will turn anxiety and nerves into excitement and confidence, as they will shift you from feeling tight and tense (threat response), to free and loose (challenge response).

Watch the video below for more on how to 'Flip the Switch':

Scan this QR Code for the Flip the Switch Video / Graphic

TAKE-ACTION STEP: Practice getting reps with the Flip the Switch routine. The more you practice it the better you will get at it and the more real it will feel for you!

Tip 4 - Visualize Past Success

This is scientifically proven to be the #1 way to feel instant confidence. Think of 5-10 highlight moments in your career where you came through in a big moment and your confidence was never higher. Got them? Now write them down.

Recalling these times will remind you what you're capable of – and what's on the other side of the slump – which will give you an extra confidence boost whenever you need it.

Think: Draw on **past** success to build confidence in the **present** to create a better **future**.

*If you have videos of these moments, create a 'Mental Movie', which is a highlight reel of you at your best that you watch right before competition to prime your mind with confidence.

TAKE-ACTION STEP: Write down 5-10 highlight moments in your career and/or create a 'Mental Movie'. Read / watch often!

Tip 5 - Your Approach Will Fix Your Mechanics

Believe it or not, slumps rarely happen because of a mechanical problem. Oftentimes it's your approach at the plate that throws off your mechanics and messes with your timing.

KNOW THIS: 99% of the time your timing will be off due to getting ready late, thinking too much, trying to do too much, or swinging at a bad pitch. None of which has to do with mechanics. Everything starts with a THOUGHT!

Which is why a consistent, rock-solid approach is usually the fix because that will keep your mechanics together. Your plan will tell your eyes what to look for in order to help organize your body to get there!

Now, what many players think is best is to hit 100's of balls in the cage after a bad game. This usually does more harm than good as you're ignoring the real issue and overworking yourself, which is stealing your energy for the next game (remember the importance of the fundamentals).

So instead of worrying about where your hands are or what your feet do at contact – focus on execution of your pre-pitch routine. In other words, think **'Execution over Expectations'**. The only thing you should 'expect' of yourself heading into competition (and during competition) is to 'execute' what is 100% in your control.

If you need to move a runner over – focus on hitting a hard ball on the ground to the right side. If there's a runner on 3rd with less than 2 outs, focus on driving a ball in the air to the outfield.

If you're popping everything up or fouling good pitches back – adjust your approach. Use mental cues like trying to hit the ball off the pitcher's foot. If you're late, focus on loading slow and early.

When you feel as if you're overthinking your mechanics and trying to get 5 hits in one at bat, approach every at bat as being 0-0 and think **K.I.S.S. - Keep It Simple Stud**.

If you want to take it a step further, write KISS under the bill of your hat as a reminder to you to slow down, and simplify your approach.

This shift in focus not only helps you get out of a slump, but fixes any mechanical problems you may be having. Know that a bad plan is better than no plan!

Some other common hitting approaches:

- See ball, hit ball
- Chose a part of the zone and only swing at pitches in that zone until you have two strikes
- Be aggressive on the fastball early in count to hit a line-drive to the opposite field
- Be patient. Track the first pitch, then look for a fastball to hit a line-drive up the middle until 2k's
- Sit on curveball, let it get deep and hit to the opposite field
- With two strikes: choke up, spread out. Think hard ground ball to the opposite field to let the ball get deep. Battle.

TAKE-ACTION STEP: Another reason hitters struggle at the plate is because they aren't seeing the ball well. What I recommend to players when they feel this way (and what I did a lot during my career) is to stand in on pitcher's bullpens. While doing it, do everything just as you would in a real game, such as your pre-pitch routine between pitches - just don't swing. This can lead you to instant improvements in how you see the ball. Give it a try!

SUMMARY

Step 1 - Master the Fundamentals of Life

- Eating: Fuel your body with high protein meals, whole foods, healthy carbs and fats, and limit sugar as much as possible.
- Sleeping: Aim for 8-10 hours in bed for at least 7-8 hours of quality sleep. Limit screen time before bed, and create an optimal sleep environment (cool temperature, minimal noise, and darkness).
- Training (Physically & Mentally): Focus on strength, explosiveness, mobility, and recovery. Go to the 'Mind Gym' for 1% of the day (14 minutes and 24 seconds) to develop your mental strength.
- Breathing: Use a 'Big League Breath' to increase your focus, manage stress and improve performance.
- Self-Discipline: Stick to your routines and do what's best for you, especially when you don't 'feel' like doing it. True self-mastery via self-discipline builds confidence and reduces slumps.

Step 2 - Accept the Truth About Slumps

- Understand that a slump is defined as not getting the desired results over an extended period.
- Accept that slumps are a natural part of the game (remember the 3 'Truths of Life'!)
- Have self-compassion to maintain a strong self-image, as how you see yourself determines how you think, act, play, and live your life.

Step 3 - Detach from Uncontrollable Goals

- Avoid focusing on getting hits, as they are outside of your control.
- Detach from personal stats and outcomes to reduce frustration and doubt.
- Recognize that focusing on uncontrollable goals leads to less enjoyment and prolonged slumps.

Step 4 - Attach to Controllable Goals

- Focus on and base your confidence on QABs: Quality At-Bats
  - Hard contact (no matter the outcome)
  - Walks and hit by pitches
  - Long at-bats (7+ pitches)
  - RBIs
  - Moving the runner
  - Sacrifice fly and/or bunt
- Shift your focus from personal success to helping your team win, which often leads to better results.

Step 5 - Develop a Pre-Pitch Routine

- Create a step-by-step routine to prepare your mind before every pitch.
- Use this routine to WIN the critical time in-between pitches.
- Stick to your routine regardless of recent performance to build consistent confidence.
- A good pre-pitch routine is a true competitive edge and will increase your odds for success. (cheat code!)

By mastering these five steps, you'll develop the mental and physical resilience needed to prevent long-lasting slumps and consistently perform at your best.

---

5 Bonus Tips to Break Out of a Slump

1) Shift Your Perspective

- Daily Gratitude Practice
  - Write down 2-5 things you're grateful for each day.
  - Focus on blessings, people, experiences, and accomplishments.
  - It is proven that this will increase happiness by 25% and shifts your mindset from negative to positive. (Attitude of Gratitude!)
- Be a Great Teammate
  - Support your teammates, especially when you're struggling.
  - Shift your focus from yourself to helping others, which builds true character and improves your outlook.

2) Define Your Best and Worst Self

- Be great with your BFS: Body Language, Focus, & Self-talk
- Assign animals, superheroes or whatever you'd like to represent your best and worst selves.
  - Best Animal: Represents your positive, confident, fearless version (e.g., lion).
  - Worst Animal: Represents your negative, timid, anxious version (e.g., sheep).

3) 3 B's to Flip the Switch

- **Big Body Language:** Assumer powerful, warrior-like posture
- **Big Breath:** Take a 'Big League Breath' to connect to your best self
- **Bring It On:** Say "Bring It On". This helps transform anxiety into excitement and confidence.
- Flip the Switch to change your mental state (confidence, attitude, self-talk, focus, body language) in the moment.

4) Visualize Past Success

- Recall and write down times when you were playing exceptionally well and pitches looked easy to hit.
- Visualize these moments or watch your 'Mental Movie' to remind yourself of your capabilities and boost your confidence before and during games.

5) Approach Will Fix Your Mechanics

- Understand that slumps are rarely due to mechanical issues alone. Instead of focusing solely on mechanics:
  - Execution Focus: Concentrate on the situational goal (e.g., moving a runner, hitting a sacrifice fly).
  - Problem-Solving Focus: Address mechanical issues by adjusting your approach (e.g., hitting the ball off the pitcher's foot if you're popping up, loading slow and early if you're late).
- This approach helps correct mechanical problems while enhancing your overall performance.

By incorporating these five bonus tips, you WILL quickly regain your confidence and snap out of slumps effectively.

We've covered a lot in this book, but before we wrap up, **I've got one last thing to ask:**

What if you could go beyond preventing slumps?

What if you could also…

✅ **Turn the fear of failure into fuel you can use to go NEXT LEVEL**
✅ **Play with confidence every game no matter the results**
✅ **Jump off the emotional rollercoaster most players ride every season**
✅ **Instantly separate yourself from 85% of players in the country**
✅ **Stand out to scouts even if you aren't the biggest, fastest or strongest**
✅ **Eliminate overthinking so you can play FREE and LOOSE on a consistent basis**
✅ **Become the absolute best version of you that there is so that you can find out how good you can be**

There's no way you wouldn't play better and have more fun, right?

That's exactly what the **Major League Mindset Program** is all about.

MLM is my 8-Week online training program that helps ballplayers win the most important game they'll ever play: **The Mental Game.**

This is your opportunity to work with me every week for 8 weeks – and learn exactly how you can start playing (and living) up to your full potential, without changing anything physically.

To date, this program has helped over 1,400 players from the big leagues all the way down to little league achieve their goals.

Here's what a few of those players have to say about their experience:

Here's everything you get access to in the 8-week MLM program:

✅ **10 LIVE Zoom Calls** with Brandon to go over each shift in depth
✅ **FREE access to HabitShare** - a habit tracking app to hold you accountable and help you create new life-changing habits
✅ **90 printable worksheets** to reinforce all 8 MLM mental shifts
✅ **FREE access to our MLM Community on Discord** to ask questions, share wins, and connect with like-minded players
✅ **Weekly competitions** to earn free MLM swag packages with wristbands, focal point stickers, medals, and more
✅ **LIFETIME ACCESS** to all recordings and resources in the program
✅ **LIFETIME ACCESS** to all future classes LIVE sessions

The next Major League Mindset Class (Class IX) begins on August 4th.

The cost of this program is $747 – but as a token of my appreciation, I'd like to offer you something special…

If you sign up for Class IX before August 1st – you can use the code **SLUMPBUSTER** at checkout for 40% off.

Whether you join us in the Major League Mindset Program or not, I can't wait to hear how this book changes your game (and life!).

Take action now. Your best season is waiting.

If you have any questions, please email me at bg@brandonguyer.com

With Gratitude,

-Brandon

Made in the USA
Middletown, DE
02 July 2024

56642224R00020